INSIDE ME

The Poetry of a Native American Woman

May you find within these pages...
something just for YOU!!

Happy Reading!!

Janette Conger

"2015"

OX

Janette Conger

outskirtspress

DENVER, COLORADO

Outskirts Press, Inc.
http://www.outskirtspress.com

ISBN: 978-1-4787-4289-0

Outskirts Press and the "OP" logo are trademarks belonging to Outskirts Press, Inc.

PRINTED IN THE UNITED STATES OF AMERICA

Dedicated to my children, Tiffanie Starr, Kristopher Dean, Hilary Rose, and Nicholas Patrick for their love, encouragement, and never ending faith in me. Your love for my writing and your belief in me, always, is what has made this book a reality. I love you. God bless you all.

CONTENTS

PART ONE
1974 - 1984

TO BE AN INDIAN

To be an Indian, is to be proud...
To be proud of who you are.
To be an Indian, is to fight...
To fight for what rightfully belongs to you.
To fight for your land and your freedom.
To be an Indian, is to know the Indian ways...
Although, as an Indian,
you don't always have to follow them.
To be an Indian is to know your tribe...
To know its place under the Great Spirit.
To know the Great Spirit,
Is of great importance...
To be an Indian.
9-4-1974

A POEM IS A POEM

A poem is a poem, as a poem will be,
To those who understand,
And to those who can see.
It has a beginning, but, never an end;
And all through my poems,
A message I send.
Read what I write, and take time to think;
What it all says,...then, let it all sink!
5-17-1978

CIRCLE OF LOVE

The never ending circle of love,
So perfect and pure, from God above.
It has its ups, and its downs;
But, only two can make it round.
It takes its time upon your heart,
Circling slowly, at the start...
Then, as each day passes by,
The never ending circle,
Is bound with love...
And receives a tie.
6-5-1978

A THOUGHT

I have to have a thought,
To get me through the day;
Without it... I cannot think!
6-5-1978

BEAUTY

Beautiful places all around,
Open your eyes, look up and down;
Beautiful things, wherever you go,
Touching your heart to help it grow;
But, don't close your eyes,
Or, you won't see...
What a beautiful world,
This world can be!
6-5-1978

THE GREAT EAGLE

Way up, high above,
Flying through the sky;
The great Eagle is free.
He searches for his prey,
Stopping only to eat;
Then, away he goes,
Through the sky,
With no feet.
Soaring higher and higher,
Circling always upward;
With no one to answer to,
The Great Eagle is free.
6-5-1978

A DEAD INDIAN

When the Indian has forgotten the music of his forefather;
When the sound of the tom-tom is no more;
When noisy jazz has drowned the melody of the flute;
He will be a dead Indian.
When from him has been taken all that is his;
All that he has visioned in nature;
All that has come to him from infinite sources;
He then, truly, will be a dead Indian.
His spirit will be gone...
And though he walk crowded streets;
He will, in truth - be dead.
9-6-1978

I AM ONE

Walking through the sand, I feel the ocean touch my feet;
I feel close to the waters.
Sitting in my backyard, I feel the sun upon my face;
I feel close to the heavens.
Hiking in the woods,
I feel branches brush against me;
I feel close to the Earth.
Standing on top of a hill,
I feel a breeze pass by me;
I feel close to the four winds.
Being alone in my special place,
The sun shining,
There is a breeze;
I sit down on the ground,
Then, it begins to rain.
I am close to all the Spirits;
I am one.
9-16-1978

GETTING HIGH

Sitting here getting high with friends,
Smoking joint after joint,
Like it never ends.
Listening to music and getting the beat;
We all sing out loud and try to compete.
Laughter, then, fills the air,
And our stomachs hurt, but, we don't care.
I ask if they'd like a little lunch,
They all dash into the kitchen;
'Cause they want to munch.
They laugh and giggle, fixing their food;
'Cause now's the time, and that's the mood.
And as each one takes their seat;
They moan and groan,
That they had too much to eat.
But, it's fun to get high,
No matter the time or place;
'Cause for some reason,
It always puts a smile on my face.
9-13-1979

A STRANGE RIDE

Walking down the street one day,
I shyly stick out my thumb;
People drive by in their cars,
Not even looking my direction.
Then, a car pulls up to a stop,
And there sits a guy.
I tell him where I'm going to,
And he says he'll gladly take me.
We drive down the road,
Neither of us saying a word;
I ask him for a cigarette,
And he offers me a beer.
We begin to talk and laugh,
Start getting to know one another;
Then, suddenly, he seems close,
Almost, as close as my brother.
9-15-1979

INFATUATION

I want to be alone to think of my life.
Where it is now, where I want it to be, and how to get there.
I try to sort out the things on my mind,
and take them one by one.
Somehow, they all seem to be related to love,
I don't know how, or what to think.
Sure, I want to give love to a special person,
And I want to be loved back.
Although, I wonder what "love" really is.
I've heard a lot about it.
How happy you always are, how good it feels
when he/she holds you, how happy you are
just being together.
Sure, it feels good when your feeling it!
But... if these wonderful feelings suddenly
disappear after a couple of months, by either one;
Well, I don't think that is "true love".
Instead, that is infatuation.
Just a road leading to love,
That turns out to be a dead end.
Oh, but, don't think infatuation is wrong! It is good...
For, at every dead end, there is a lesson to be learned...
Either, about ones self, or, about the world around you.
THINK ABOUT IT!
11-17-1979

LIVE AND LEARN

The past is what we've learned,
The future still lays ahead;
Yesterday is gone.
And today has still to be lived.
10-21-1980

I THANK YOU

When we had no where else to go,
You gave us a home and food to eat;
Just when we thought that no one cared,
You showed us that you were there;
For this...I thank you.
When I felt that I could go on no longer,
You helped to give me strength;
You showed me that I could make it on my own.
For this...I thank you.
Even though you had troubles of your own,
You never once burdened me with them;
Instead, you opened your home to us,
And gave us everything you had.
Only asking of me to help myself with my life;
For this...I thank you.
You've given us so much, that to repay you
would take a lifetime.
So, for you, I would like to give something
to last a lifetime.
My friendship and my love...
Both of which are true and last a lifetime;
I pray that you accept.
I thank you.
11-30-1982

LOOKING BACK

For years I have written poems,
And every once in a while I go back and read them.
Just now, reading them made me feel strange.
When I wrote some of these poems, I didn't
quite understand why I had.
But now, to read them, its as if they all have
a certain meaning to a part of my life that
hadn't existed then.
Its like my life up to now is right there
in front of me.
When I go back and read them, I understand them
in a way I never had before.
I just can't explain what an experience it was.
I guess it's time to start a new chapter.
12-5-1982

FEELING CHANGE

I've been through a lot these past few months.
Things have happened that I never thought could have.
I've felt so many different feelings.
Some I didn't even want to feel.
Yet, there they were.
So, I pushed them away.
I tried so hard not to let them touch my life.
But still, because of these feelings;
My whole life has changed.
12-5-1982

MY PRAYER

I pray that you'll watch over me and mine;
Help me to trust you no matter what the problem.
Give me strength to cope with all that hurts me.
I pray that you will give me understanding of
what's happening to me;
For I know you have the answers and I must
always believe that.
I thank you, Jesus, for your love for me;
And for the sacrifice you made so that I may
be free of sin;
Most of all, I thank you for coming into
my heart, and giving me a new life.
12-8-1982

A GIVING GOD

Your strength is my strength;
Your love is my love;
You've given me answers,
When I had none.
You've taken my problems away.
You lifted the burdens from my shoulders;
You gave to me a new way.
12-9-1982

YOU CAN SURVIVE

Sometimes, you just want to end it all,
But, you know you can survive;
Putting it all in the back of your mind.
At times it seems so hard,
Trying not to think;
Of how it all happened,
And taking one day at a time.
You wonder if there's anyone,
Who really understands;
What it is your going through,
Because you know you don't.
All you know is that you can survive,
And you must...
So, you set new goals,
And life goes on.
7-4-1983

FEELING YOU

I feel so secure when I'm with you.
And so lonely when I'm not.
You are my sunshine on rainy days.
You make me laugh,
When I want to cry.
It seems that you are always there,
When I need you most.
Just feeling your touch,
Let's me know you still care.
Please don't stop or go away.
Not today, not ever.
7-4-1984

YOU STILL HAVE YOU

I wake up to a bright sunny day,
Not a cloud in the sky.
It makes me realize things aren't so bad.
You have to be grateful for what you have.
Even if you have nothing...
You still have YOU!
7-4-1984

I GAVE YOU IT ALL

When I gave you my love, I gave you it all.
I did not keep some for myself.
I gave you it all.
For, I knew you could appreciate it,
And not take it for granted;
Yet, still return all that you receive.
So, when I gave you my love,
I gave you it all.
7-4-1984

A ROSE

Just a rose upon the table,
It looks so real, although, it isn't.
You want to pick it up and smell its
fragrance,
But, there is none.
So, you just look at it,
Enjoying its beauty, and its serenity.
Knowing that it will never die.
Knowing way down inside,
That you will.
7-4-1984

FOR A GOOD DAY

Here's a hug - here's a kiss,
To help get you through your day.
If it doesn't -
Don't you fret...
There's plenty more on the way.
7-6-1984

THE JUDGE SAID PAY

The Judge was a hard ass,
He was mean as a rat;
He yelled, "You go to Shelton!"
And that was that.
Oh, he told that Judge,
As he walked away,
"I'll serve the time,
But, I won't pay!"
So, there he is at Shelton,
Just a serving' time;
He had to leave his woman,
And his child behind.
And when he gets out,
He'll be out to stay.
And never, again, to go away.
8-30-1984

LOSING YOU

How long I have waited,
To hear you say I do;
And more than I can count,
There are ways that I love you.
How long has it taken us,
To join our hearts together;
And have peace and contentment,
It must have been forever.
There were times when you,
Wanted to get away and to be free;
Of household chores, debts, children,
And yes, away from me.
Women's lib and equal rights,
Seemed to get in our way;
Somehow, we made it through,
And at last, we're happy today.
But, oh, how long will your heart be happy,
How long will you be true?
For, you're away from home so much,
I'm afraid of losing you.
9-6-1984

KEEP AMERICA CLEAN

Friday comes, the eagle flies,
The sky is red with flames;
Far away a baby cries,
A country sits in shame.
Death bells toll, a widow weeps,
Box-bearers shuffle past;
A hero lies in silent sleep,
A flag is flown half-mast.
Another soldier goes to fight,
As blood and guts flow free;
He, too, will die, perhaps tonight,
"...sweet land of liberty."
The thunderous roar of booming guns,
A charred and tattered city;
Bodies rotting in the sun,
Who are we to pity?
Stiff white shirts and tails,
Long black limousines;
Wash the blood from 'neath your nails,
Keep America clean.
9-17-1984

MOTHER

There you lay so still and quiet,
Not a worry in the world for you;
I want to cry way down inside,
But, you said you didn't want me to.
How could I have taken for granted,
All that you said and did?
And never realize all it meant,
Until after, you were dead.
You taught me how to be a lady,
How to love, how to laugh, and understand;
And if you had not taught me all this,
I would not know when to lend a hand.
All the things you gave to me,
I still treasure in my heart;
Even if I don't have those things,
In my life, you're still a part.
I want you to know I appreciate you,
Just for being my Mother;
And I know that in this whole wide world,
I can never find another.
9-21-1984

LIFE THROUGH LOVE

I sit here knowing,
That inside of me is life;
And life through love,
Is a gift from God above.
Can we really pretend,
That we don't care?
And treat it as if,
Its just like the air?
We can walk away,
And hope it isn't so,
But, way down, deep inside,
Both of us know.
9-26-1984

BOOK OF MEMORIES

Within my book of memories,
Are special thoughts of you;
And all the many nice things,
You so often say and do...
As I turn the pages,
And recall each single thought;
I realize the happiness,
That knowing you has brought...
The memories of the times we've shared,
Both bright and gloomy days;
Are memories of your kindness,
And your friendly, thoughtful ways...
There are memories of your laughter,
Your gay and cheery smile;
That add a bright note to each day,
And make my life worthwhile...
There are memories of the things we planned,
Each friendly little chat;
When we would get together,
And talk of this and that...
When I recall these memories,
As I go along life's way;
I find they grow more precious still, with every passing day.
10-10-1984

IF ONLY

If only...you could see into my heart,
and know exactly how I feel.
If only...you could feel my emotions,
and know the depth they come from.
If only...saying to you "I care",
could tell you more than that.
If only...you knew how much I care,
without me having to say it.
If only...you could hear my thoughts,
and know what I was thinking.
If only...my love could embrace you,
as the universe does the Earth.
If only...saying the words "I love you",
told you just how very much.
If only...I could give you my love,
in a way I never have before.
Yes, if only...
10-20-1984

EMPTY AND ALONE

Oh babe, how I miss you,
When you're away from home;
The house feels so empty,
And I, so all alone.
I turn on the t.v.,
Watch a little bit,
Or, even go to sleep.
I'll go to visit friends,
And take drives to anywhere;
But, its just not the same,
Cuz babe, you're not there.
Oh yes, I want to be with you,
Where ever you may be;
Cuz my heart, it feels so lonely,
When you're away from me.
Please come back soon,
From where ever you are;
And I'll be here waiting,
No matter how long.
10-26-1984

LIFE'S NOT EASY

All of us were babies,
Dependent as could be;
On parents to provide for us,
All our wants and needs.
As we got a little older,
Our only thoughts were of toys;
We dreamed of Christmas, birthdays ,
and presents,
But, hadn't yet thought of boys.
As teenagers we started finding out,
How life was going to be;
We wanted so badly to grow up,
That the hardships we couldn't see.
Now that we've grown into adults,
And struggle to get through each day,
We pray to God for help and strength,
As we go along life's way.
Everyone says it's a part of life,
Yes, growing up is hard to do;
Some might think its an easy thing,
But, you and I, we have to.
11-4-1984

OUR LOVE

Please don't turn away from me,
Please don't ever go astray;
Honey, I love you so very much,
I really do want you to stay.
Help me to not hold on so tight,
Help me to give you some room,
For, if this is what you want and need;
I hope it will help our love bloom.
Give me a reason to keep on going,
Give me a reason to fight;
For, at the end of this deep dark tunnel;
Somewhere, there's got to be light!
Say our love will grow each day,
Say our love's that strong;
You know, the days go by so slow,
And the nights just seem so long.
Tell me this isn't permanent,
Tell me this isn't the way its going to be;
Let me know I'm in your thoughts,
And that you will always love me.
11-4-1984

WRITING TO YOU

I take my pen and write to you,
When I'm down and feeling sad;
And after just a line or two,
Things don't seem so bad.
As I write each line down,
From deep within my heart;
I know your in my thoughts,
Even when were far apart.
And as I go on writing more,
My feelings get honest and true;
And then, only after a while,
I don't feel quite so blue.
Writing to you makes me feel better,
Both on the inside and the out;
If you don't know I'm writing to you,
By now, you should have no doubt.
11-4-1984

PART TWO
1985 - 1995

SOMETHING FOR NOTHING

You have a song upon your heart;
And its one that you want to share.
Its all about love, about giving and sharing;
And receiving nothing in return.
Your Father once told you, when you were young;
That you never receive something for nothing.
"How can that be?" you ask yourself;
As you grow up, and learn about love.
Now, you're not talking about a physical love;
Or, a love that is blinded by lust.
You're talking about a real true kind of love;
That's given from the heart and is free.
For, you have found,
That when you receive this kind of love;
You're truly getting something for nothing.
1-31-1985

SIT AND THINK

I sit here and think. About what?
I don't know.
Just thoughts running through my mind;
About this, that -n- the other.
They just come and go,
Don't stop for very long;
Just linger in my mind,
And then, their gone.
Oh yes, my thoughts are many,
Racing back and forth;
Taking only just a little minute,
To simply let me think.
They go so fast about in my mind;
I hardly have time before they leave me behind.
So, I'll let them go as fast as they will;
And grasp what I can...
While I sit here and think.
2-19-1985

THE OLD

The old, they have so much to teach,
The young, who do not know;
Way down inside,
Within their hearts;
If you look... you'll find a show.
The old, they want to share with you,
The young, all you do not know.
The wisdom they've gained,
The knowledge they have;
If you look... you'll find a show.
2-19-1985

I REMEMBER

I remember when we first met,
Two years ago, today.
We laughed and talked,
Told jokes and drank;
Then, both went our separate ways.
At that time, I didn't know if
I would ever see you again,
Or, what would ever become of that day.
And when I did see you again, and again,
I knew I never wanted to let you go.
I'm glad I never did.
I remember the first time you told me
"I love you",
I had to look into your eyes to know that
it was true.
As I did, my heart was filled with such joy.
It was at that moment, that I, too,
realized how much I loved you.
And in that same moment, I also realized,
That a love like ours could do nothing,
But, grow stronger and stronger,
With every day that passed.
And so it has.
3-2-1985

A SNOWFLAKE AND ME

A snowflake upon my window sill,
I look at it just knowing;
That there is not another like it,
Even when it is snowing.
When I look into a mirror,
The one thing that I see;
Is a person, so unique,
Staring back at me.
Just like a snowflake from the sky,
I, too, was specially made;
I, to live an dwell on Earth,
The snowflake, to melt and fade.
As the flakes fall to the ground,
I know that they can't be;
Anything else, but flakes of snow,
For, that is all I see.
Looking in the mirror, again,
What do you think I see?
Yes, that person, so unique,
I know it can only be me.
3-20-1985

BE WITH ME

You are my strength when I feel weak,
And yes, I need you at a time like this.
I've always had faith that You are by my side;
My problem I share with you,
For, I know that with You, there will
only be the truth.
I have done nothing wrong.
I just don't understand.
I only ask that You be with me,
To hold my hand, or carry me;
Whichever I need.
I want to know that You are by my side;
No one else will do.
Thank you for Your love.
5-4-1985

FRIENDS

F - is for the FIGHTS we had,
and still, friends we remained.
R - is for the REASONS why,
we were told to stay away.
I - is for the INSTINCT we share of knowing
when we are needed.
E - is for EVERY time we sat over coffee,
talking and laughing,
about this and that.
N - is for the NEED we have to know
where the other is at.
D - is for the DISTANCE in miles
that won't ever keep us apart.
S - is for the SMILES we have on our faces
whenever we think
of one another.
When I put all the letters together it spells 'FRIENDS'.
A relationship that's so special and dear,
no one can take it away.
9-17-1986

A.C.O.A.

How can I be someone else's strength,
Yet, not have enough strength for myself?
How can I truly love another person,
Yet, have no love for my own being?
Why, can I give to others,
Yet, not be able to receive the same?
Because I don't know how!
10-11-1986

WHY ME?

"Why me?"
It's a question everyone asks themselves,
at least once in their lives.
Now, I find myself asking that very
same question...
"Why me?"
What am I suppose to learn, or get, from all
this hardship that has been thrown my way?
Still, I must continue to be strong.
I know that because I keep waking up to a new day.
I must go on.
Once again, "Why me?"
I look around at the people in my life,
And see sickness everywhere...even death.
None has touched me.
Not even a cold could get me down.
My children, my Dad, my sisters, my friend.
"Why me?"
Why all around me, yet, not me?
I don't understand.
Maybe one day...God will let me know.
Then, I won't have to wonder.
Or, ask "Why me?"
2-10-1988

MY LITTLE BABY GIRL

Though she was just a baby,
Her strength she had to share;
And way down deep inside myself,
It was strength I had to bear.
She gave her strength so freely,
How could I not accept this gift?
With my feelings so mixed up and confused,
It was her strength, that gave me a lift.
I waited and waited,
Each day, praying for word from above;
And during that time, my baby girl taught me,
Patience, faith, and love.
Soon, the day came to be,
That she was well enough to go;
And picking her up in my arms,
From her face, her virtues did show.
It was from my little baby girl,
That I had learned so much;
She reached out to me, from a hospital bed,
And my whole life is what she touched.
2-23-1988

RECOVERY

I sit here now, not alone;
Just by myself.
Knowing that my mind is clear,
To think my thoughts;
And my heart is able ,
To feel my feelings.
Though, I have been violated,
Beaten and bruised,
Still, I am standing;
And will continue to stand,
Tall and strong.
For, my spirit is growing;
My wounds, healing, slowly...
With a positiveness,
That I know can only be from within.
9-22-1988

SOBRIETY

My life now is called sobriety,
And oh, how good it feels!
To have a mind that's able to think,
Instead of one, that is crushed by heels.
Deep inside, I had dug a hole,
That now is beginning to fill;
With clean, healthy, positive things,
My hole shall become a hill.
I'll have to work very hard,
Sifting through the good and bad;
In the end, I know I'll have,
The best life I've ever had.
No one can take away from me,
What I have given to myself;
That's a life of sobriety,
Not, one that sits on a shelf.
9-25-1988

IN - BETWEEN

With my life somewhat peaceful,
Still, my mind wanders;
From the past, to the present
Then, into the future.
Remembering and learning.
It's good for me!
Yet, it will be work I'll do,
To keep my pace.
Just where I'll end up, is hard to say;
But, I do know that it will be a place,
Where I'll want to stay.
9-25-1988

DADDY AND ME

Daddy, I miss you, each and every day;
I remember the way we used to laugh and play.
I know you're not with me anymore, here on Earth;
But Daddy, I thank you, for helping with my birth.
Now, I am searching to be born, again;
To find myself and who I am.
I've never forgotten the words you told me.
That "when life gets tough, to have faith and believe";
"Never stop believing" was what you said to me.
Then, taking my hand in yours,
You placed in my palm, a small silver case,
lined in red velvet;
Enclosed inside was a small silver Mother Mary.
I stared at it for a long time,
then closed my hand around it,
And we hugged.
What a beautiful memory you gave to me.
I love you, Daddy, even though you're not here;
Yet, I'll have all the memories,
And in each one we will be;
So, I can never forget - Daddy and me.
10-6-1988

MY GOD

MY GOD - has a <u>BRAIN</u> that thinks of my needs
before I have a chance to.

MY GOD - has <u>KNOWLEDGE</u> of my pains, and will
take them away, should I want it.

MY GOD - has <u>EYES</u> that see the good in me and the
worth that I have.

MY GOD - has a <u>HEART</u> that will give me the kind of
love, understanding, and compassion that
I also find in myself.

MY GOD - has <u>ARMS</u> that wrap around me, or carry
me, whichever I need and where ever I
need.

MY GOD - has <u>LEGS</u> that have traveled down my
path, clearing away rocks and brush, so
that I will not stumble and fall.

MY GOD - has <u>FEET</u> that have walked many miles
before me, to know what is ahead of me.

MY GOD - has the <u>POWER</u> to give to me what I
cannot give to myself, whether it be
forgiveness, honesty, or trust.

This is <u>MY GOD</u>. Now, I must begin to bring this spirit
to life...within myself.

10-10-1988

THE CHILD I WAS

So many times I look back on my life,
Seeing ugly an hurtful things.
My heart tugs at me,
To pull away from what I see.
Yet, I know now, just how real
the feelings are.
I try now, to feel the feelings,
Of hurt and pain...
Knowing how deep they are,
I want to know it wasn't my fault...
Still, I feel like it was.
What to do about all this,
Is something I continue to contemplate;
Knowing I have been SO violated,
I try not to let it happen, again.
And I know I can do it!
Because now, I'm no longer...the vulnerable child,
That I was - before.
10-16-1988

ALL THERE IS OF ME

When I can't give all that is wanted by another,
Or, can't say what is wanting to be heard;
Nor, feel deep enough to share;
Then, all I have, is what there is of me.
When I don't give in to guilt and shame;
Or, try taking control of others lives;
Nor, accept responsibility for actions that are not mine;
Then, what I have, is all that there is of me.
So, I can't change another persons being,
Or, give away something I don't have;
Nor, keep what is not mine;
But, what I have, is all that there is of me.
10-19-1988

CHANGES -N- ME

Changes make the world go 'round,
They make me grow inside;
Some are good,
Some are bad;
Oh, the changes that I've had!
There are times when I look ahead,
And see changes coming on;
Knowing there is nothing I can do,
So, inside I try to stay strong.
Waiting for a change is hard,
But, its something I must do.
'Cause when a change is finally over,
I always know that it was suppose to.
4-17-1989

A GOLD SPIDER

A gold spider came down on me one day.
I snatched its web - looked at it;
Then, let it be on its way.
Mom always said gold spiders,
Meant you were going to get money.
If its true, then, I'm due.
How will I know?
We'll see, my dear...only time can tell and show.
6-17-1989

A LITTLE BOY'S SLEEP

My little boy is not going to sleep.
Bribery? It doesn't work.
I've tried it.
"Wanna go to the park?"
"I have a surprise for you when you wake up."
It seems nothing works.
What is a Mother to do?
"Go to bed!" I yell.
Into his room he goes.
Out he comes, again!
Finally, he stops fighting,
Many hours later.
First, the yawn -
Then, the quietness...
Suddenly, he has fallen to sleep.
7-4-1989

TO YOU - MY FRIEND

I know that you are troubled,
I see tears flowing from within;
You needn't worry, though, my friend,
Because now you can begin.
To give yourself a fresh new start,
Putting away hurt and pain;
Even though, shut doors may open,
Your strength will close them, again.
If you search deep down inside,
You'll find beauty, strength, and hope;
Hold on, dear friend, don't let go,
For, this is how you cope.
You'll find in time the tears will fade,
The troubles may go, too;
And when they rear their ugly head -
You'll know exactly what to do!
So, be patient, my friend,
After every darkness, there is light;
Know inside that you can do it.
I think you'll be all right!
Strength, courage, and wisdom,
To you - my friend.
8-9-1989

A DREAM OF PEACE

Peace.
What is peace?
Is it listening,
And having an open mind?
Giving and sharing,
All that we have;
Until others feel contentment,
In their own lives?
We'll never know,
Unless we try;
Reaching out our hands to one another.
That the hope for peace,
Can be more than a dream;
For dreams do come true.
Peace, my friend,
Is what this brings;
Peace, from me to you.
9-2-1989

GOOD-NIGHT, MY LOVE

I walk up the stairs,
Then, hesitate, halfway up;
Turning, I look into your eyes,
I see real love deep within,
You begin walking toward me.
I shake my head to say "No";
You stop in your tracks;
We pause.
I slowly kiss my hand,
Then, blow the kiss to you.
You reach for me.
My hand reaches for you.
I turn, slowly,
Continuing up the stairs;
My hand dragging on the rail;
I try to keep eye contact.
Then, you disappear.
9-20-1989

MIRROR TO MY SOUL

As I gaze into the mirror of my soul,
I see a vastness within myself;
That I have never known.
Peering at its contents,
The haze becomes overwhelming;
I stare into the openness,
Of my soul that's been shut-out.
With intent and yearning,
To know what's going on;
I reason and rationalize,
Those little parts of me;
I see, but do not understand.
But, if I continue diligently,
My mind absorbs what ever I find;
Giving off sporadic light,
To the vast haziness of my soul.
Time will then do its part,
For haze, will give way to light;
And I will see within myself,
The me, I left behind.
10-28-1989

THOUGHTS OF TOUCH

My mind wanders with endless thought,
As a yearning burns deep within;
My soul reaches out,
To touch, and want;
Oh, the desire.
The thoughts rush in, then out,
Leaving feelings all alone;
A warmth surrounds my being,
As my mind races;
To yet, another thought.
With all that happens,
My heart is still;
A thought grabs me,
Holding me tight;
And then...
Touch.
11-24-1989

A NIGHT SPENT

As your hand runs down curves,
That have been left alone;
You send me to heights of ecstasy,
I let go of a long time ago.
With your lips you take me in,
Keep me, and hold me;
My mind melts into the moment,
Then, I feel your touch, again...
With the movement of my hips,
I draw in the tenderness;
And yes, the desire...
Of the one who knows gentleness,
and intimacy.
As you push deep into my being,
I open my soul and let you in;
With knowing inside, I take all of you,
This sending chills down my spine - and a
tingling at the nape.
Having reached this height of a pleasure unfelt,
I lay in your arms and my inner thighs quiver...
Knowing it was you who brought me where I am,
In this moment.
11-26-1989

THE DARK SIDE

It's called the dark side.
The sun never shows its face to those doors.
The people who live there, live day to day.
Getting along with each other, yet, in their own worlds.
There's a light of good versus evil.
The battle never ends.
Oh, the dark side -
A breezeway that's called the gateway to hell.
Enter into what is here.
Taking part, is of your choice.
You don't even have to stay,
And you will never escape.
1-31-1990

SLEEPING BABES

When the children are asleep,
The house is so quiet that I don't know what to do.
After a while, I go in and check on them.
I see their closed eyes and hear the sounds of
restful breathing.
I pull their covers up over their shoulders.
Then, kiss them on the cheek.
As I walk out the door, I turn,
Look at them, again...
I remember their innocents, their dependence upon me;
And the joy my children bring into my life, each and
every day.
Now, all the love within me,
Reaches out to them;
Touching their sleeping heads.
I turn and leave the room,
Knowing that they are all right.
3-12-1990

LEAVE MY DOORS ALONE

I hear your words,
Not knowing what to think;
You don't even know me,
Nor, do I, you.
With words you push buttons inside me.
Then, red flags raise up.
Why?
It's not easy for me,
To open doors within myself;
That have been shut, locked,
And now, have no key.
Yet, you push me up to the door,
Even putting my hand on the knob;
You haven't a clue,
Why I don't want to hear you.
Why I push you back,
Asking that you turn around;
And walk away,
Leaving me alone.
6-14-1990

QUESTIONS OF SELF

I prayed to the Heavens above,
Asking for forgiveness, and love;
For feelings I don't understand,
And love, well, I wonder.
Is it in me?
Somehow, I know it is.
Where?
I want happiness.
Yet, wonder what it consist of,
Not knowing if I have found it,
Or, if I have let it go.
Can anyone know what it is I'm feeling?
How far away are we from each other?
And why? No fault.
Cause? Who knows.
Just care and love.
Always to you, my friend;
Where ever you may be.
8-10-1990

I DO REMEMBER

Where are you now?
How far away are you from me?
I can't even touch you.
Though, I do remember.
What are you doing now?
Cooing, laughing, crying?
Are you content?
I can't hear you, baby.
Though, I do remember.
What are you thinking?
It was that I could tell,
Just by looking;
I can't see you, baby.
Though, I do remember.
Remembering now, is all I have,
Each memory being put away in a chest;
Hoping that we will be together, again,
Though, I will always remember.
9-6-1990

UNKNOWING LOVE

As fear takes over the innermost part of my being;
I try to look onward without hesitation.
Yet, still something pulls at me.
I constantly push it away,
With a lingering of the unknown,
Also, within my soul.
I ask questions that get no answers,
At least, not yet.
And as the fear subsides for only a while,
I take this time to catch my breath;
And believe that all will be right.
Yet, deep within my soul,
Fear is ever-lingering, unwilling to let go.
The hours pass by one by one,
And with each that goes,
Is the growing need to know;
Just what the outcome will be.
For now, I will sit and accept,
What comes from within...and so be it.
10-10-1990

THOUGHTS OF YOU

Sitting here, thinking of you,
Wondering exactly where you are;
And what you are doing this instant.
Are you thinking of me, too?
Right at this same moment?
I don't know what your thoughts may be,
But, I can tell you, the thoughts within me.
My thoughts are of you,
Of our times together;
Your smile, and your face.
How the warmth and love,
You have within your soul;
Are always felt by me,
During the day and the night,
I think of you.
I know this is something more
than I can control.
So, I just let all the love flow.
Sitting here, with thoughts of you.
10-24-1990

YOU ARE MY PATH

As I walk down this path of life,
I'm glad you are by my side;
Holding my hand, assuring me;
With every step I take,
That you are next to me.
Your understanding and
continuing love,
Help me to heal, every time I
stumble and fall;
As I walk down this path of life.
10-24-1990

FRIENDS SUCH AS US

Friends such as us were meant to be.
Me for you, and you for me.
I have something to give you,
You, something for me.
Love, comfort, and laughter?
Its gotta be all three.
Without you as a part of my life,
Is like the Universe without Earth;
Or, the sky without stars.
Someday we will realize,
How lucky we really are;
Friends such as us,
Hold dear to our hearts;
A bond that can never die...
Even when we're far apart.
9-10-1991

LIFE'S CHANGES

Just as the seasons change,
So does life;
Taking you through good times,
And times of strife.
You may not be able to tell,
When a change will occur;
It may be way down deep,
Or, it could just be a blur.
Life has a way of changing,
And you'll have no control;
So, when life does this to you,
Just take the punch and roll.
It may hurt a little bit,
But, be strong, and see it through;
No change could be so bad,
That it needs to destroy you.
Take heart! Chin up!
Changes happen for a reason;
For, that is life -
It's just like the seasons.
9-18-1991

LOOKING FOR PEACE

It's okay to be angry,
It's okay to hurt;
It's okay to feel your feelings,
But then...let them go.
Do not keep them,
Do not let them linger;
Do not hold them close to you,
Just let them...go away.
If peace is what you're seeking,
Then this, you must do -
Feel the feeling,
Acknowledge the feeling;
Then...relinquish the feeling.
Peace be with you...
Always.
3-4-1992

OF MY CHOICE

Some doors close,
Only, so that other doors may open;
It is my choice, as to which doors stay closed,
And of the open ones, which I'll pass through.
With expectations and anticipation held high,
Passing through open doors,
Can be like that of fighting a losing battle.
Knowing the choice is mine,
Whether good or bad;
Every open door is a chance for me;
To grow, learn, and experience life.
At my own pace, and of my own choice,
I'll pass through the open doors,
Sometimes, quickly...sometimes, slowly...
But, always...of my choice.
6-2-1992

HOW FAR AWAY ARE YOU?

Tonight I wonder if You are here,
Though, I know You would not be far away;
'Cause every time I think You're gone,
You always reappear.
You know when I need You,
And when I'm in despair;
You gave all You have for me,
Long ago, without a care.
Yet, now I sit and wonder,
How far away You can be;
Little do I know,
You are not far away from me.
You show Your presence every day,
Even, if I do not see;
Somehow, You let me know,
You are always here with me.
When things get hard,
It's to You that I pray;
And I wait so patiently,
For what You have to say.
Cause I know I cannot do it,
On my very own;
I must give thanks to You, dear Lord;
For all that I am.
11-12-1992

THIS PLACE WE CALL HOME

Oh, the trees that surround me, as I look out the window;
No cars with loud engines, nor, sirens to keep peace,
or, help others.
I see the sky with its many moods,
And hear birds chirping in the woods;
Watching the trees sway in the wind,
I give into my minds wondering thoughts.
Feeling the cold seep through my clothes,
In this drafty place we call home;
I sit close to the wood stove,
And I know the cold won't last long.
There's wood stacked for the winter,
Just waiting to be burned;
I remember how much work it took,
When the weather was nice and warm.
At times a plane will fly over,
Reminding me that people are here;
That they are not too far away,
Should I want or need them near.
Yet, in the quietness that is out here,
And in the solitude that I have;
The desire for another's company,
Only distracts me from the wondrous beauty,
Of this place we call home.
2-23-1993

FATHER IN HEAVEN

I sit here now, feeling things I thought were gone long ago.
I'm flooded with emotions,
The tears won't stop;
Confusion and wonder cloud my mind.
I try to find comfort with my Father in Heaven;
Still, the tears and pain won't stop.
I want to be angry, but the hurt won't let me.
So, I cry some more...my eyes are swollen, my mind tired.
I want someone to listen, and know that no one hears me;
Except for my Father in Heaven.
Why?
I do the best I can with what I have.
I guess its just not enough.
Oh, my Father in Heaven...
Please hear my crying, and wipe away my tears.
I ask that You hold me close to You;
To forgive me for any pain I may cause.
I'm so sorry - please forgive me.
My Father in Heaven,
Please.
8-1-1993

FOR THE MOMENT

In the quietness of the house,
I sit alone and listen.
My mind never stops going;
It's like listening to someone,
Who never stops talking.
With so much to do around the house,
My mind constantly reminds me of it.
None of which, I really want to do,
But, I know I must.
I only wanted to stop for a moment,
To write some of my thoughts down.
10-4-1993

MOTHER TO MOTHER

Shunka- a dog.
Within her there is life.
As I look into her soft brown eyes,
I can see fear.
She trembles.
Knowing it is time to let go,
She goes into her house.
I wait.
Then, I go to her.
I see - not just a dog,
But, a Mother,
Caring for her newborn.
Inside, knowing how she must feel.
She stops what she is doing,
Looking up to me, only for a moment;
Her eyes, now ask for reassurance.
Mother to Mother...
I simply smile, then, nod.
And so, she continues her work.
11-11-1993

CHALLENGE

To have challenge in ones life is what keeps one going.
It's not the challenge, itself, that matters, but how you meet
that challenge that makes the difference.
Challenges come into a person's life to help them grow.
Facing challenge and learning from
it can change ones perspective
about life itself.
It takes inner strength and courage to overcome challenge.
There is no room for self-criticism.
Turn away, or give up, and you could lose
a part of yourself that
you may never find again.
Challenges aren't meant to be easy,
but they come into ones life for a reason.
When the reason is clear,
the challenge can be attacked with full force.
For then, one will know what is needed, to overcome
the obstacles that stand in the way of challenge.
11-11-1993

WE ALL FALL SHORT

We all have things we are <u>THANKFUL</u> for,
Some are big and some are small.
To always <u>REMEMBER</u>, is the challenge
we fall short of.
We all are <u>ABLE</u> to give freely,
Of our words and angry feelings.
To always <u>THINK FIRST</u>, is the challenge
we fall short of.
We all <u>WANT</u> to feel fulfilled,
In one way or another.
To always <u>HAVE LOVE WITHIN</u>, is the challenge
we fall short of.
We all have the <u>DESIRE</u> to be loved,
By another human being.
To always <u>LOVE OTHERS</u> is the challenge
we fall short of.
We all "CAN" remember.
We all "KNOW HOW" to think first.
We all "DO" have love within us.
We all "HAVE THE ABILITY" to love others.
Yet, these are the challenges,
We all fall short of.
11-30-1993

A MESSAGE FOR MY SON

Oh, my baby Kristopher,
So young and full of life;
I write these poems,
For you to read,
When you're grown -
And have a wife.
Oh yes, my little darling,
I know you cannot read;
But, one day you will read these words,
And know just what they mean.
Oh, how I hope that you will find the me,
You'll go away and leave behind;
Search within my words, dear child,
And see what you can find.
Oh, the messages that I have written,
Are for you to pass on;
It's all up to you, my son,
For, one day, I will be gone.
1-15-1994

YOUR LOVE FOR ME

Oh, how much I love you,
For those little things you do;
That tiny peck upon my cheek,
Can only mean 'I love you'.
Bringing to me flowers,
Or, a card when I am blue;
Show me that you care for me,
More than anyone else could.
The gentle brush against me,
That slap upon my rear;
Tell me more about your love,
Than any spoken words would.
The touching of your hand in mine,
That stare from a distance;
Sends a message loud and clear,
How could I resist it?
It's your arms around my waist,
As I'm standing at the sink;
Your gentle kissing on my neck,
Making me stop and think.
It's the shiver down my spine,
And those chills all over me;
That wants your love even deeper,
Than it could ever be.
Showing me how much I'm loved,
With actions, instead of words;
Let's me feel it's safe to say,
These very special words...
"I love you!"
1-16-1994

WHO AM I?

When I start to wonder,
Just who it is I am;
Then, I know it's time,
To begin that fearless search again.
To look deep within myself,
Finding parts of me I never knew;
Makes me ask myself a question,
That must have an honest answer;
Do I really want to?
Not waiting for my reply,
Curiosity, slowly engulfs me;
As my need to know rises to a
peak of overwhelming;
And I sit, silently, in confusion,
With each new part of me;
Screaming out to be heard.
Finally, I step forward,
Take each part one by one;
Pick at it carefully,
And accept what is there;
Without a single word,
About what it is I see.
I can feel strength and courage,
There by my side;

Waiting for me to grab hold of them,
Should I want to run and hide.
Yet, I know that with the passing of time,
My still unknown parts,
Won't hit with such a wham!
I'll get to know my person inside,
And not have to wonder, anymore -
Who it is I am.
1-16-1994

MY DEAR OLD FRIEND

We met when I was just a kid,
My friend, you're always there for me.
You've listened, tolerated, cared about,
accepted, loved and given;
These things you did not only for me,
but, for others, too.
You became more than just a friend to me,
You were, and still are, a part of me.
For many years we did not see, or talk
to each other,
Yet, thoughts of you would keep coming
to my mind;
I didn't know where it was you were at,
Or, if there were many miles between us,
holding you back.
I searched everywhere I could think of,
wanting to know where you were.
Then, one day it happened, and we were
together, again!
Now, with only a few hours drive between us,
It seems we seldom have time anymore,
To be with each other, the way we were before.
We've grown up, old friend,
A family and responsibilities take up our
time, now.
We find ourselves having to *make* time for us;
A few minutes on the phone, a cup of coffee
and a chat,

Or, a letter written, telling of this and that.
Though, there have been more letters than I can count,
They pull us together when one of us is falling apart;
Knowing the time spent writing, gives strength to
our friendship,
By keeping us close to one another - be it only
in the heart.
So, if one day, you should get a letter from me,
That rambles on and on, without really
saying anything;
Don't sit there and wonder what is going on,
Just read it, again, for an old friend's sake.
Look not at the words, but at what's written
behind them,
For, it's you, my friend, who sometimes knows
me better than I know myself.
So, I'm counting on you now, and I haven't
any doubt;
That you will be able to see inside me,
And know what the letters about...
Oh yes, my dear, old friend,
I *was* feeling blue, and simply that means -
I've been missing you.
1-21-1994

MY CHILDREN'S LOVE

As I awoke one early morn,
Three children stood by my bed;
One was crying, one was calling,
And the other wanted fed.
It wasn't even light out yet,
So, I offered them my bed;
But, one by one, they went out the door,
And my eyes slowly closed, again,
Before my feet could touch the floor.
More sleep was what I needed,
I only hoped they understood;
I never even stopped to think,
That maybe, they just would!
When I woke up for the second time,
And got up out of bed;
I went down the hallway, then stopped,
Without one word being said.
I saw that my three had gotten dressed,
And my oldest son was getting the other two fed;
Each had a bowl and spoon in front of them,
The cereal and milk were out, too;
So, I stayed where I was,
Quietly watching, just to see;
If they would get along,
Or, if they needed me.
Whispers and "shh" was all I could hear them say,
They didn't fight, laugh, or even play;
Then, suddenly, it dawned on me -
That's right, I thought!
It's Mother's Day!
1-30-1994

TEARS OF DEPRESSION

The tears won't stop flowing down my cheeks,
Though, I wipe each one away;
I can feel depression coming on,
No matter what I have to say.
I talk out loud to myself,
Yet, it doesn't help one little bit;
My feelings keep swirling around in my head,
Then, passing by my heart, taking a piece of it.
I don't understand why this is happening.
How are my tears making a puddle on the floor?
I couldn't have been crying that much!
Now, there's a knocking at the door.
Frozen with numbness, I'll stay sitting in this chair.
Who's at the door? I really don't care.
Oh yes, the knocking continues, a few minutes more,
But, I'm not about to open that door!
So, the door wasn't opened,
And I never did find out;
Just who was doing the knocking, or, what it was about.
Finally, the tears and depression left me.
I've come a long, long way;
Now, I'm able to feel the way I do today,
Full of peace and contentment,
I'm very glad to say!
1-31-1994

MY LITTLE ONES

Oh, my two - five and four,
How could I want , even one more?!
Yet, every day that passes by,
As I look into their faces;
I know why.
At times they are wild,
And fight all day long;
Or, whiny and picky,
Not eating dinner at all.
And though nap times are harder,
Than they used to be;
I know it doesn't mean,
That they don't love me.
It's just that they are growing,
And so fast, I must say!
That the color of my hair,
Is turning from brunette to gray.
But, if it wasn't for my little two,
I'd have no life at all;
Cause I just love to watch them,
As they grow from small to tall.
2-2-1994

I DO THIS FOR YOU

You may think that I don't care,
But, God knows that isn't true;
It hurts me so very much,
To have to say "NO" to you.
I want you to please understand,
This is the way it has to be;
That soon, it won't be just us two,
Instead, it will be us, three.
If I open my door to you,
And let you in my home;
How will you learn to make it?
To stand up on your own.
I can't push away all I have now,
So, I can give to you, from me;
Cause if I do, and let it all go,
Then, just where will I be?
To you, this may sound selfish,
If it does, well, that's okay;
Cause your life is your own,
And learning from it, is the only way.
2-2-1994

A DAD'S TIME TO GO

His time has come,
And now he must leave;
You have to let him go,
Not wanting to, you grieve.
As his name is being called,
One last breath he'll take;
Now, you must learn to live your life,
For you, instead of, for his sake.
Know that he is leaving behind,
A spirit for living life;
And a strength that can endure,
No matter what the cause of strife.
So, to him, you bid farewell,
Knowing he won't be far away;
Within yourself, you'll see parts of him,
Or, you'll hear his voice in something you say.
You'll hold close to your heart,
Whatever parts of him you find;
So, you will always remember the Dad,
Who was gentle, loving, and kind.
You tell him to go now, and be at peace,
That it's time for him to rest;
And very deep inside your soul,
Will be the place he did his best.
2-3-1994

YOUR SOUL'S ANCHOR

With so many things going on in your life,
Your soul searches for an anchor;
That one place where it can settle,
Undisturbed.
Where all that happens will simply
flow right over,
Leaving your anchor in its spot of
desired contentment,
And your whole being can feel assured;
That the anchor will forever be,
Untouched.
4-11-1994

BOTTLED UP INSIDE

Pain and hurt.
Tears.
Uncontrollable crying.
Sleep?
Only from exhaustion.
Yearning with wonder.
What am I to do?
Continue in the misery;
Knowing I don't have to?
Am I wrong?
More pain.
More hurt?
Why?
And if there's a God in Heaven,
I ask for courage and wisdom;
For, I am blinded by confusion.
What am I to do?
Where's the light?
I need my peace within.
I really am...so scared.
5-30-1994

SEASHELLS OF THE OCEAN

Seashells of the ocean,
Entice me with your essence;
Speak quietly to my silent soul,
Tenderly, hug the thoughts,
Deep within my heart.
Bring yourselves upon me gently,
Whenever, I am alone.
Oh, channel whelk of simplicity,
And moon-shell of solitude;
Remind me softly to always refill my cup.
Teach me, seashells of the ocean,
With a radiance, I know not;
How the double-sunrise can reflect,
A purity of love in a relationship;
To validate our time *alone*,
Yet, together.
Whisper to me seashells,
So that, we, two, may bond;
By letting each other live freely,
Without hesitation -
And hold lightly, not clinging,
So, that growth can be found;
Just as the oyster bed,
To the rock, with its shell.
Seashells of the ocean,
Your essence will be within;
When thoughts from my heart tug quietly,
And without relent;
I'll put you all in my hand,
Hold on to you gently;
And reminisce of our time spent,
Alone.
6-23-1994

SMILES OF PLEASURE

Lips, tenderly desire,
As hands caress the skin.
With penetration into my place,
Of tightness, I take you in;
The pleasure being felt,
Leaves emotions far behind.
Overwhelmed, by excitement,
Ecstasy, takes over;
And slowly, we see and feel,
A smile...
Both, yours and mine.
8-9-1994

WITHOUT A GUARANTEE

There's a fear inside me,
Making me want to cry;
Because I know that without my child,
I have no guarantee.
I ask myself a question,
That has but one answer;
The question?
Am I willing to go through it, again?
The answer. No.
The fear is real!
The tears, I can't hold back,
Knowing there is only one thing for me to do;
Bring my child back to me,
Give him love;
And help him to understand.
What else could I possibly do?
Without a guarantee.
8-15-1994

DREAMING OF PASSION

I sit here now,
With thoughts of you;
Running through my mind.
Wanting just to touch you,
And press my lips to your body;
I ache to feel your hands,
Caress me in my nakedness;
As I lay next to you.
A yearning now engulfs me.
My thoughts continue on.
Our legs entwined together,
You pull me even closer.
My hand reaches for your place of desire.
Then, I feel the warmth of our bodies,
Collide with one another;
Into a passion,
Felt, once before.
Yes, the want.
Oh, the ache.
Please, fill me, once again.
8-31-1994

TWENTY YEARS AGO

To Indian Heritage High School,
We dedicate this night;
For, it was twenty years ago,
The beginning of our plight.
With just a handful of students,
And a staff that really cared;
We learned about our cultures,
And about the land we shared.
We chose the Eagle as our mascot,
Wore the colors of green and gold;
Then, put together basketball teams,
So, our heritage we could show.
One by one, the years passed on,
And graduating class numbers grew;
We've even had to say good-bye,
To some dedicated staff members, too.
So now, let us gather together,
Each and everyone, to celebrate;
The survival of Indian Heritage,
With yet, another, open gate.
9-10-1994

PART THREE
1995 - 2015

MY CHILD IS FOUND

It was so many years ago,
That you left my very side;
And though, I fought and struggled to keep you,
I had to let you go.
I didn't want to give you up,
It was the hardest thing for me to do;
I ache and longed to have you back,
I'd even cry myself to sleep, for you.
I kept hope and faith in my heart always,
For, I knew one day you'd be back;
Though, I never knew when, or how
it would happen;
To dream seemed to be enough.
Dreaming helped me to hold on tight,
To the hope and faith I had inside.
It is by God's grace,
I don't have any doubt;
That we found each other,
With our arms now, stretched out.
The tears that fall from my eyes,
Are not those of sadness, anymore;
But, are tears so full of joy,
Because I'll have all my children with me;
Finally, I'll have all four,
Back with me, again.
7-7-1997

THE SUN IN MY SOUL

Rays of sun beat down on me,
A smile of warmth, I can feel;
Going deep down into my inner soul,
I reach out for even more.
Wrapping myself up in it,
My soul screams out to me,
As I sit, basking in the rays of warmth,
With no one to bother me.
There are noises all around me,
Though, I do not hear them;
For, the quietness, now surrounding my soul,
Soothes my mind...
While the warmth of the sun,
Engulfs me...even, into my very soul.
9-2-1997

ROSES I SEND YOU

Your gentleness, I can feel,
Just by reading your words;
Roses, I will send you,
For the garden you have grown.
It's many colors will reflect,
The friendship and smiles that we share;
Even though, many miles keep us apart,
Your garden of roses will always be there.
The abundance of roses in your garden,
Will never diminish;
Just as you will never...
Be gone from my heart.
I'll keep you close, and hold you dear,
Today, and always;
For, when you are not here to talk to me,
I feel a tugging at my heart;
And my soul cries out,
To read your words, again...
And so, roses I send you.
10-10-1997

A ROSE COLORED SHOWER

He walks through the bathroom door,
Water is running...the shower is on;
From behind the rose patterned curtain,
He can see her figure.
Her long hair flowing over her small, petite body,
Slowly, he begins to undress,
as he watches her every movement;
From behind the rose patterned curtain,
He wants to be with her.
Opening the curtain, he smiles, and steps inside.
Her tan, sullen brown skin tone, he embraces with his eyes.
He notices not, the smile upon his face;
As he slowly takes in all of her,
With his touch...kiss...and caress.
Her hands touch him all over, covering him with soap;
"Washing you" she says, as she places the bar in his hand;
He slides the soap over her skin,
feeling such pleasure and honor,
to be the one enjoying this.
She picks up a bottle and takes his hand in hers,
Pouring a pearly pink liquid into his palm.
Shampoo.
He rubs his hands together, then, places them upon her head.
The lather - and her hair...so long and full;
They smile at each other, then kiss, not wanting to stop,
but, do anyway.
Standing back, he watches as the lather runs down her body,
Making her look sleek, and sexy;
He then, steps forward...another kiss, as he helps her
with her hair.
Taken away by a single kiss, they let the water fall upon them,
As they take each other in, deep into their souls.

The water still runs on them, as they stand;
Closely embracing one another,
Basking in the passion and sensuality of the moment.
Not wanting to leave this moment,
Knowing that they must;
And so, they do.
11-21-1997

WITH YOU, FOREVER

I want to reach for you,
Because I feel I need you.
I yearn for your touch,
Because it is something I haven't
felt in a long time;
The touch of a loving man.
I ache to be with you,
Because with you, I can always
feel love.
I desire you to be in my life,
Because without you, my life would
never be the same, again.
With laughter and love,
You make me shine...
With you, is where I want to be,
Forever.
3-2-1998

GIVEN GIFTS

The many miles between us,
All things said and done.
I see now, how unique we are,
For my path is of red.
Clearly, I was given gifts,
Of words, and of wisdom;
Yet, not to keep, but to share.
Still, some won't know,
That the giving of gifts;
Has purpose in itself.
If not for ones self,
Then, for the ones receiving,
Should they be able,
To hear with their heart.
8-10-1998

ONE SPIRIT - ONE HEART

On this day so blessed,
We all gather here with you;
Letting you know we'll guide,
And support, all you do.
Deep within our hearts,
You'll see our spirits soar;
As we send you on a journey,
Together, now as One.
Our hope for you both, is happiness,
May "bliss" always be there, too;
Though, there will be times of trial,
Know that God, will see you through.
Hold each other always,
Hand in hand, heart to heart;
Joined together, now you are,
To stay One in Spirit...
And never again, to be apart.
9-1-1998

MY NIGHT MOON

Upon the sky, you sit.
Your brightness giving light,
To all the creatures below.
I look up to you, with stars all around,
And can see your face,
Smiling upon me;
Oh, my night moon.
My spirit soars to you,
Mesmerized by your beauty,
You hold me...
Entice me...
Until I give my heart away;
Yes, to you,
My night moon.
11-4-1998

NATIVE BROTHER

He came upon me like a mist in the night,
A glow I could see, deep within his soul;
With his words he embraced me,
Until I wanted to hear even more.
A closeness I could feel,
His spirit touched mine;
The bond was created.
A connection made.
With an inner spirit,
He is, my Native Brother.
11-5-1998

NATIVE SISTER

My Native Sister?
Who is she, you ask?
She is someone special who can feel my joys, sorrows,
and hurts...
She is someone, with whom I can do the same.
We are connected by our hearts.
With our eyes, we can see into each others souls,
and know who we are.
We have the kind of arms that wrap around
one another,
Whenever one of us wants to be comforted;
This is done with a sisters love.
Our legs will carry us, always, to each other,
Whether it's walking, or, to run to;
Should the other have a need.
Yet, during those times when we are apart,
My Native Sister is never far away;
For, all I have to do, is close my eyes,
To know that she is by my side.
11-5-1998

FINDING ONE TO LOVE

I have to get out of where I am.
I've got to begin to do what is right.
I need someone to love,
Who can and will love me, too;
Will I ever find this person?
Who can he be, and where is he?
One day, maybe, we will find each other;
Then, I won't have to be lonely, anymore.
11-7-1998

NO ONE TO HOLD ME

To be held in someone's arms,
Lovingly, and with care;
Instead of sitting alone, watching t.v.
As an emptiness surrounds me,
I realize that I have no one;
To listen to me, or, to be with...
No one to just hold me.
11-8-1998

SOMEONE TO LOVE

I want to love someone,
With all that I am;
And be loved back,
The same way.
I want someone to care enough,
To want me not to cry, anymore.
I want to show how deep I am,
How much I care;
And that my love is real...
Knowing all the time,
That I must be, just me!
11-8-1998

WAITING FOR THE ONE

From deep within me,
I know feelings are there.
Some I've felt before,
Others, I've kept at arms length;
Not wanting to be hurt, again,
Or, told that I am wrong.
I'll just continue on...
Waiting for the right one.
But, how will I know?
When he has truly come.
11-8-1998

A YOUNG LADY TO BE

A young lady of an age not yet grown,
Trying to have a place in the group, of her very own.
Not knowing how to show it,
The words to relay are hidden from her mind.
So, with her hands and feet,
She lashes out to be seen, and yes, heard.
To teach her is my job,
A young lady, with respect for self;
Knowing that inside she's seeking,
Attention and love.
Wanting it badly, she wonders how.
With feelings confusing her,
She does what she thinks will work,
Without considering how it will look;
She cares only about how she feels.
A Mother to her, I am.
Wanting her to understand;
She's at an age now, where feelings run wild;
That one day she will not be, just a child...
She'll look into a mirror,
And there she will see,
A young lady whose grown...
Into all she wants to be.
2-4-2000

SPIRIT BEINGS

Spirit Beings, from beyond,
Protect me, make me strong.
Give me your wisdom,
That I may see;
Show me the path,
You've cleared for me.
With your breath,
Clear my senses,
Down to my very soul;
So, I may hear, see, and feel,
The way that I must go.
Spirit Beings, from beyond,
Never leave me alone.
Surround me, keep me,
Make my star shone.
Bring out from within me,
The parts of you,
For others to see;
All the Spirit, within me.
5-26-2002

MY LOVE, YOU KNOW

To tell you how much I love you,
I cannot put into words.
You are on my mind always.
You never go away.
I feel your presence in my every thought.
Knowing you are here with me,
There's a smile on my heart.
I hope you feel it, too,
Way down in your heart and soul;
All the love I have for you,
For, this is what I want you to know.
11-5-2004

CHILDREN OF THE STREET

Children running amok in the streets,
What's this world getting to be?
What is it, that we want to leave behind?
Is it wild children without a mind?
You tell them you love them,
You give them things they want;
And make sure they have what they need.
Then, there are the ones you feed.
It's sad, but, true.
One day, our children will rule.
How will they do it?
With guns and anger all around?
As they run in the streets,
Without any ground,
Hoping one day to be found?
They're children...they're *our* children;
Those children of the streets.
6-25-05

OUR ONE-EYED MAN AND HE/SHE

Our one eyed man, and he/she,
Came into our lives wantin' a fight;
We sent them on their way,
And they came back the very next night.
Apologies were given and taken,
New friends, we all became;
Now, he/she sits behind bars,
And the one-eyed man, ain't the same.
So, the trailer title is up for bail,
And he/she gets to come back home;
Now, the one-eyed man,
He doesn't have to sleep alone.
It's breakfast for dinner tonight,
The one-eyed man has his he/she;
And every time you read this,
Know that it came from *ME/ME*!
9-5-07

THIS IS ME

No one can tell me who to be,
If I want to be myself;
For, who I am,
Is all you will see;
This is who I am...
This is me.
My feelings are true,
My heart is real;
And I want to say thanks,
For letting me show,
Just how it is I feel.
I tried not to burden you,
As your Mother and your friend,
I asked only of your shoulder;
So that I could talk or cry,
If only for a moment.
My greatest gift is to listen,
With smiles and hugs that are free;
Know that my spirit is with you,
For, this is who I am...
This is me.
4-4-2009

TO MY DAUGHTER

You may not be *my* Mother,
Though, a Mother, you are, too;
And I want to take this special day,
To say how proud I am of you.
We may have our spats now and then,
As all Mother's and daughters do;
Yet, as I listen to your voice and words,
I learn so much more about you.
My pride in you is overwhelming,
For every task and challenge you endure;
I can see my own strengths and courage,
Of this you can be sure.
I watch from a distance, as you grow stronger,
And admire your spirit, as no other;
For, I feel the loving heart and soul,
Of a daughter, sister, wife, and Mother.
You warm my heart, inside and out,
Every time I laugh with you;
Yet, the best part of knowing another Mother like you,
Is also...having a best friend, too!
3-29-2011

THE WONDER OF THINGS

Looking out into the world, I wonder many things...
Like why we fight amongst ourselves,
While other countries fight, just to be free?
Or, how we can say we care about our homeless;
Yet, still kick them aside, to the curbs of our streets?
And what will become of this world when we're gone?
What does the *next* generation think?
When will the people of this world come together,
To save this place...the Earth, *our* planet?
Who will stand up with a resounding voice,
To let others know, the world has a choice?
And where will you, or, I be...
Should this world finally find peace?
These are some of the questions I ask,
As I watch the world...and wonder many things.
4-12-2011

EYES IN THE WORLD

Eyes are everywhere,
No matter where you look.
What the eyes see...
I can see flowers of many different colors,
Showing off their colors to anyone who
wants to take a minute;
And enjoy the scent, as well.
Eyes of the world...
What do your eyes see?
11-5-2011

PEACE AND LOVE

Peace to one side, love to the other.
Peace not being without love,
Nor, love without peace.
Let each dwell within your heart.
Then, spread your peace and love,
Like wildfire to others.
Spread your wings and fly.
Let no one bring you down,
From the place you soar to;
When you go to your place,
Of peace and love.
12-4-2011

THE MEASURE OF AN AGE

It's every age that is measured,
By what has been accomplished;
The lessons that have been learned,
With challenges that have been endured.
From the beginning of an age to the end,
Each deed done is measured;
Not by a spoon, or, even a cup,
But, by the power of intention.
Every age is its own to live through,
With deeds of every kind being done;
Yet, the measure at the end of each age,
Is something that's never thought of.
Know that your measures will be added together,
At the time of your last breath;
And let your deeds be honest and true,
Right up, until your death.
12-8-2011

A PLACE OF PEACE

Peace is a place inside you that only you know about.
It is up to you whether or not to share your place of peace.
Going to your place of peace can help you to become more
calm, no matter what the strife.
Let no anger enter into your thoughts or your being,
For, this will only cause upheaval.
Keep your place of peace free of bad or hurtful ideas.
Inside yourself, feel the freedom *real* peace can bring.
Accept too, the spirit of peace,
And then, give it to another.
Find serenity within the quietness;
Then, you will have a place of peace,
That is your very own.
12-8-2011

PEACE AND LOVE

Peace is being content with yourself and who you are.
Love is giving of yourself without conditions.
Peace is having no anger within, or around you.
Love is caring about what happens to others.
Peace means no wars with others.
Love never gives up when the going gets tough.
Peace is feeling a calmness inside your being.
Love is received in the same portion that it is given.
Peace and love are both alive and well,
Entwined together within the soul;
Waiting to be set free and to roam,
Around the world so they can grow.
Will you, and can you, do your part to help?
Let each and every person spread the word,
Of peace and love.
12-9-2011

SELDOM YET OFTEN

It's seldom seen,
yet, often felt.
It's seldom given,
yet, often received.
It's seldom wanted,
yet, often possessed.
It's seldom accepted,
yet, often needed.
It's seldom heard,
yet, often spoken.
It's seldom forgiven,
yet, often accused.
It's seldom grieved,
yet, often remembered.
It's seldom known,
yet, often thought.
It's seldom traveled,
yet, often lived.
It's seldom over,
yet, often ended.
It's all of the above, rolled into one.
It's seldom...yet, often.
12-16-2011

THE WORLD THROUGH RAINDROPS

On a stool, sitting at a window,
Elbows on sill, chin in hand;
I wipe away the dew from a small square pane of glass,
Only to look out through raindrops, at a world, distorted.
My sight being blurred, I think of the poverty,
Of governments and their people colliding in war;
World-wide, being unable to see what is real,
The images run into one another.
Each raindrop hits the glass, and gathers
together with others,
Growing in size, they run down toward the pane;
And like all people living in poverty world-wide,
They blend in with the rest...and become survivors.
Headlights of white blaring through the raindrops,
Leaving only streaks of red passing by;
Reminding me of those who haven't the time,
To be a willing part of a solution.
Just as rain drops fall down upon the windows,
And gather together as one;
So, does the burden of poverty fall upon its people,
As they gather in large numbers just to be heard.
It's through raindrops,
That I look at the world...from a window.
12-18-2011

ANGELIC-LIKE SENSATIONS

To believe that there are angels among us, is one thing...
Yet, has it ever seemed like there really is an angel in your life?
Did you know that that angel is you?
You'll feel and recognize the angelic like sensations flowing
through your spirit and your being, when in certain situations.
You'll know it when sharing your events in life with others,
And them commenting on the aura of goodness
that surrounds you.
It's when your giving of the gifts within you to others,
and they, too,
can feel the joy you have inside you when doing so.
It's being accepting and giving of love to and from others,
unconditionally,
that gives to the pureness of heart that every angel has.
It's when doing a good deed for someone,
without expecting anything in return.
The sensation you feel inside can be like you're
floating in the air.
Inside each and every one of you, there is an angel.
It is up to each of you, individually, as to whether
or not, the angel inside will flutter it's wings,
or, let the glow of its halo be shown.
When you can let your angel walk beside you
on your path in life...
Then, you will know that you are *truly* blessed.
1-14-2012

PAIN WITHIN

I hear the words "emotional pain"
and remember things that are quickly
put back away. Yet, the words stick with me.
Emotional pain. What is it
to me? It's not being able to be me, nor,
being able to go places, or, do
things all by myself. It's a feeling inside me
that I'm not sure about
because I've been told that it's not good to feel.
I may feel alone sometimes, yet,
at the same time I can feel within
myself a need to let it be known.
There are times when I want to talk, but,
don't know what to say.
It's like being all alone with nothing.
I'm hurting and lashing out on all that is around me.
I don't know who I am
anymore, and feel like I'm losing
a battle I didn't even know I was fighting.
Emotional pain is what I feel when I'm being told
how *stupid* or *dumb* I am.
Or, when I do something and it makes me feel good inside,
only to be told
that what I did was done the wrong way, or,
for the wrong reason.
The emotional conflict that this causes is
an inner pain that's hidden deep
inside my soul and begging to get out.
I cannot let another person keep
me from doing the things that I have been gifted with.
I can hang on to my
emotions, turning my heart away from the hurt...but still,

there's the inner
conflict and pain that needs to be faced.
I cannot let my being shy away from the challenge, but must
let my spirit stand strong, as I face and conquer the challenge;
For, this will only strengthen my spiritual being.
1-18-2012

OUR SPIRIT OF LOVE

A love like we have never known before,
Given and received, unconditionally;
Is a love that penetrates deeply,
Taking us to levels that have always been there.
It's the love that's between us,
Along with a calmness that overtakes us;
That let's our spirits relax,
Knowing it's love we give to each other;
For, our love inside gives the same to all,
who touch our spirit.
Let your spirit touch our love,
For, it is given to you to be received;
Freely, and without condition,
To all who touch your spirit, too.
11-7-2012

A DAY OF HOMELESSNESS

Waking up to roll a cigarette, if you have one, and smoke,
Load up your backpack and put everything in its place;
Lift the backpack onto your back...adjust.
Take a deep breath of fresh morning air,
Let it out slowly...then, the walk begins.
To do what needs to be done,
To survive, yet, another day;
Needing food, needing water,
Some, needing a drink, too;
Nowadays, a phone to charge,
Is also, on the list to do.
With community meals served
throughout the day,
Along with bags of food to go;
All can be found and done in a day,
Even, if surviving, humbly alone.
A place to lay your head at night,
Where you won't be hurt, and feel safe;
Is the last thing on the list you keep,
As you check it off...and fall asleep.
8-12-2013

IN THE MEANTIME

"In the meantime"...what do we do?
Keep on loving, though guards are up;
Live, learn, and love,
From within it all will come.
All the love you will ever need, or want,
Is all ready there with you;
Deep inside your being,
Is the place you can find love.
"In the meantime"...
clean your body,
clean your house...
find love within.
11-13-2013

UNICORN OF MY SOUL

Unicorn of my soul,
Tame my inner being;
Give to me your courage,
So, that I may go forward;
Into places unknown,
Without fear.
Unicorn of my soul,
With your strength, keep me strong;
So, that I am able to endure,
All that I am faced with in this world.
Unicorn of my soul,
Share with me, the majesty that is you;
When confusion surrounds me,
Holding me down;
Lift my spirit unto you,
And raise my head high, once again.
Unicorn of my soul,
With your alicorn, let your wisdom be
known to me;
So, that I, too, can see within my soul,
That which is both, you and me.
12-6-2013

MY SILENCE FOR WEAKNESS

Though I sit quietly,
Looking around;
At where I am,
Without words,
I know that my silence is good.
For, with silence comes the knowledge,
That no one else can see;
And that I give to myself,
Inner strength - that which is inside me.
With silence - I hold strong.
Do not mistake my silence for weakness.
1-29-2014

TO ALL THOSE WHO COME TO SEE ME

Thank you.
I know you're here.
I can feel you.
Remember me...hold my hand.
It's okay to touch me,
Or, talk to me;
I hear you, still.
I know you are here.
Say goodbye, if you must,
Know, I will always see you;
For, I will be watching over,
Always letting you know I'm there.
Remember me with smiles and laughter,
The same as I always gave to you;
For, there is no sorrow greater than this...
The having to say goodbye.
3-4-2014

LION AND UNICORN

I am born unto the lion,
With all its traits, I roam;
Looking for my Pride,
The ones I call home.

I am the spirit of the unicorn,
Whose strength, courage, and purpose;
Are given unto me,
That I may forge on;
Forever dwelling in the hearts,
Of those who believe.
4-3-2014

DEEP INTO MY SOUL

It's every thought within my mind,
Screaming to get out;
Yet, my silence gives me strength,
Deep into my soul.
Reaching out, I clutch at strength,
With courage;
Unyielding, I bend.
Wanting nothing more,
Than the thoughts within my mind;
To give wisdom to my heart,
Touching me, inside,
Deep into my soul.
Just hold me and let me cry;
Cleanse me with your power,
Great Spirit...
Deep into my soul.
5-14-2014

TO ALL WHO WILL LISTEN

Let it be known that Mother Earth is hurting.
She does not want you to poke her with the needles,
you call drills.
Her blood, is your oil...the Sun, is her Brother.
Her Brother wants to help us,
If we would only listen.
He tells us there's another way.
When will we listen to our Mother Earth?
And to her Brother, the Sun?
No, to pipelines being layed out, like i.v.'s through
our Mother Earth's veins...
No...to continuing her pain.
Our Mother Earth cries out to the only ones who
can save her.
Yes, you...the human being.
5-14-2014

THE FIVE ANIMALS OF EARTH

There is a strong spirit among the animals these days.
They are bonding together, for each other...
A lion, a tiger, a bear,
Growing up together thirteen years;
Inseparable.
A ten year old goat,
Lost and dying for his life long friend,
the burrow...
Both showed love, when reunited;
Though, they are very different...
They see only the spirit of the soul.
The Creator has placed blessings upon
these chosen animals,
That they may be able to show us...the caretakers,
How to share, how to accept;
And how to love without condition.
The Great Spirit can see the greatest challenge
we are faced with...
The ability of the caretakers, worldwide,
To just get along and love each other.
Let there be peace.
Blessings to all.
5-26-2014

RED ROAD

Walking the Red Road gives challenge to my soul,
To know and find myself, as I was created;
The Red Road challenges me to walk through
my past, and *not* stay...
But, to forgive, and be forgiven.
On the Red Road I am ever reminded,
That the day I am in,
Was given to me for a reason;
That I may be able to find a piece of myself,
Hidden away deep inside.
All the while, the Red Road will widen as I walk,
So, that others may walk with me;
To hold hands, listen, or, to give a hug;
For, the Red Road is not just for one.
6-2-2014

HE AROSE

It's our Lord Jesus Christ who was risen,
To forgive our errors and to give love;
Not just for one of us, but, for all,
For, His gifts come from above.
Knowing just what He was doing,
Jesus Christ gave His life by shedding His blood;
He then, arose for each and every one,
So, that our errors would be gone.
His love forgives all errors,
No matter how great they may be;
Because His love is unconditional,
Ask for it...you'll see.
Our Lord Jesus Christ asks only of you to hear Him,
To read His words and to pray;
His arms are wide open to forgive you,
Whatever the time of day.
Take in the love that is offered,
Have your errors wiped away;
Know you've been forgiven,
And that His love is there to stay.
8-5-2014

HER CHILDREN

Sad for one child,
Happy for the other;
The feelings deep inside,
The heart of a Mother.
As one child cries,
The other has opening eyes;
The ones pain is self-inflicted,
While the other, sees only the future.
Knowing the ones tears and pain,
The Mother's arms are open wide;
To receive the other, once again,
Into her folds and by her side.
The Mother knows the one will grow,
For, with change comes knowledge of self;
The other will blossom and bloom,
Though, she'll need a little help.
Hoping the one child will stay strong,
In the midst of challenges coming her way;
The other will be planting a garden,
To give flowers to friends, one day.
The Mother quietly sits watching both,
As they live their lives with change;
Her heart sad for one child,
Her heart happy for the other.
8-10-2014

SIT WITH ME

I sit with me,
Yet, I am not alone;
My thoughts are there keeping me company,
In quietness, my emotions flow.
Alone with me,
Thoughts of every kind;
Feelings being free to roam,
Giving in to me, I let them go.
Sitting alone with me,
My company of thoughts;
Helps my spirit to stay strong,
In quietness, I am not alone.
11-20-2014

OUR DEAR THERESA

Your smile could brighten anyone's day,
Your laughter is still being heard;
We didn't know the depth of your pain,
You never said a word.
Your joyous spirit will live forever,
In the hearts of those who are here;
Each time we feel a warmth, or, a chill,
We'll always know you are near.
An angel you are, now in heaven,
Watching over us each and every day;
Letting us know you're happy and safe,
And that all your pain has gone away.
Though, you're reasons we may never understand,
And your life with us here, cut short;
Our love for you will always be here,
In our memories and the stories we tell.
We'll know that it's your beautiful face,
Beaming down on us from above;
When we see the sparkle of a star,
Or, the full moon's face of love.
It's so hard to say goodbye to you,
So, instead we'll say "Till we meet, again...";
Rest peaceful now, our dear Theresa,
In God's house, forever... Amen.
12-20-2014

RAIN IN SEATTLE

It's a rainy day in Seattle.
What are you to do?
Walk in it...
Be happy that the rain gives to the trees,
And plants of Mother Earth;
For, she must be thirsty,
Our beautiful, Mother Earth.
Let the rain cleanse your soul as you walk.
Feel it's gentleness upon you.
Let it run down your face;
From the top of your head,
To the tip of your nose,
Then, let it drip...
Deep into your being.
Thank you, God and Creator.
12-23-2014

SUICIDE

Dedicated to my niece, Theresa Ella Slow Barnes R.I.P.

Suicide.
It's effects, rippling,
Into the heart and emotions;
With a depth like no other...
Like a knife shoved deep into the soul.
Suicide.
Each ripple holds within,
A memory, a tear, a pain...
And answers unknown;
Like a searing fire that leaves only ashes.
Suicide.
To some the only answer,
For problems nobody knew...
Thinking no one would understand;
Like the light of a candle,
Blown into darkness;
Quickly, gone.
It's effects, rippling...
Suicide.
1-8-2015

WHAT SPIDER?

I saw a small spider come down upon me,
As I was looking in the mirror one morning.
I watched, as it worked its way down;
Then stopped, and sat right in my face.
I looked at it some more...from all angles.
Could swear it was hanging there,
Just staring at me, too.
Now, I don't like spiders much,
And really big ones scare me.
But, this little 'ol spider just hanging there;
Maybe begging for its life;
Tugged at my heart, making me smile.
So, I took it by its web, straight to the front door.
Gave it a good toss over the railing,
And said, "Get out! Live! Don't come back!"
Feeling good for not killing it...
I closed the front door, went back to the mirror;
And smiled at myself, again.
1-21-2015

THE END

CPSIA information can be obtained
at www.ICGtesting.com
Printed in the USA
FSOW01n1139060715
8547FS